The Running of the Bulls

Michelle Lee

World's Greatest Celebrations: The Running of the Bulls

Copyright © 2017

Published by Scobre Educational

Written by Michelle Lee

Scobre Educational
42982 Osgood Road
Fremont, CA 94539

www.scobre.com
info@scobre.com

Scobre Educational publications may be purchased for
educational, business, or sales promotional use.

Cover and Layout by Sara Radka
Edited by Lauren Dupuis-Perez
Copyedited by Malia Green
Images sourced from iStock, Shutterstock, Alamy, and Newscom

ISBN: 978-1-62920-576-2 (hardcover)
ISBN: 978-1-62920-575-5 (eBook)

Table of Contents

Introduction

The running of the bulls is a **tradition** in many cities across Spain. The most famous city where this event takes place is Pamplona. Pamplona is in the Spanish region of Navarre and has many bull-running races during the San Fermín festival. The festival takes place each year from July 6 to 14. It is an eight-day celebration to honor San Fermín, the saint of Navarre. The party is filled with singing, dancing, and fireworks. It is all about fun, excitement, bravery, and danger.

The bulls are released onto the streets!

Did you know?

In Spanish, the running of the bulls is called *encierro* [en see air oh].

The dangerous part of the festival is the running of the bulls. Each morning, the bulls are led out of their pen and released onto the streets of Pamplona. Rocket guns are fired to let everyone know that the bulls have entered. A short distance ahead of the pen, some of the bravest people are lined up.

Once the shots have been fired, the runners begin to run as fast as they can. They have 825 meters (2,707 feet) to cover with charging bulls chasing after them. Crowds watch on the sidelines, cheering for the runners to make it safely to the finish line. Most races take three or four minutes, and those minutes are an exciting and frightening experience for the runners. If you can't keep up with the bulls, then you'd better get out of the way!

Runners watch out for charging bulls.

History

The running of the bulls is part of a festival that is hundreds of years old. Many **Spaniards** are Christians, so the festival has religious meaning. It begins with the story of Saint Fermín. In the 3rd century, Pamplona was a Roman city. Fermín was a bishop who wanted to share his knowledge of Jesus Christ. Fermín's teachings turned thousands of people into followers, but the Romans did not like this and had him killed. Since then, he has become a hero and saint to the people of Pamplona. To honor him, the San Fermín festival is celebrated.

In the **Middle Ages**, the festival had **bullfighting** and took place in October, but many people did not like the bad weather and so the celebration was moved to the summer. In the 16th century, there were more activities added, such as music, theater, dance, **fairs**, and fireworks.

DID YOU KNOW?

The Pamplona bull runs have many rules to protect runners. Only adults 18 or older can participate in the bull runs and runners must wear the right clothes and footwear for the race. Shopkeepers and homeowners are also warned not to leave their door open if their property is near the path of the bulls.

From the 17th to 18th centuries, the festival became bigger with acrobats and **tournaments**. This is also the time when bull-running began to happen. **Drovers** would gather the bulls into a herd and lead them to the ring so that they could be released for the bullfights. Over time, people thought it was more exciting to run with the bulls instead of just leading them from behind. Bull running was also a chance for young people to show off their strength and bravery.

The running of the bulls is celebrated to honor Saint Fermín.

In the 19th century, people from around the world started coming to the festival. There were circus performances—like a woman being shot from a cannon—and animals from far-away lands on display. There was also the *Comparsa de Gigantes*, or Parade of Giants. During this time, the bull runs were very exciting, but more dangerous than today. There were no fences around the running course, so sometimes bulls would escape and run freely through the streets, crashing into things and harming people along the way.

A double fence keeps the audience safe.

Today, the running of the bulls is world-famous. People from all over the world come to run with the bulls. It is now much safer than it used to be. There is a double fence along the racecourse so that bulls do not escape and harm the audience. There is also a large team of doctors, nurses, and Red Cross **volunteers** that are ready to help any runners that get hurt during the race.

The running of the bulls can be a very dangerous sport.

In recent times, the running of the bulls has been questioned by the public. Some people find the sport too dangerous because of the many runners that get hurt each year. Although it is rare, people have also died from the bull runs. Sometimes the bulls get too wild and strike people with their horns. Or sometimes people fall and get crushed from the weight of other runners. In the last 100 years, 13 people have died in the Pamplona bull runs.

A bull charges at a matador's cape during a bullfight.

Other people think that the bull runs are cruel to the animals because they are being led to the arena for the bullfights—a time when Spanish **matadors** fight the bulls to the death. Each year, **animal rights activists** gather before the festival to **protest** the bullfights. Aside from the bullfights, Spaniards have great respect for the bulls during the runs. Taunting, teasing, or harming them is not allowed and Spaniards even find it insulting when someone hurts the animals during the races.

Runners and bulls run through the streets of Pamplona.

The Colors of the Running of the Bulls

Red represents the people of Biscay, a Basque province in Spain.

White represents faith.

Blue represents the color of the heavens.

Green represents the oak tree of Gernika, a symbol of Basque freedom.

Location

The city of Pamplona is home to nearly 200,000 people.

Spain is a country at the southwestern tip of Europe. It is neighbors with Andorra, France, and Portugal. Spain is also located near the African countries of Morocco and Algeria. Since it is close to so many places, it is not surprising that Spain is rich in culture and history. For example, Arabs from Africa influenced Spanish music. They brought the guitar and flamenco dance to Spain, and now the country is famous for its elegant flamenco dancing and classical guitar playing.

DID YOU KNOW?

Although located in Spain, the Basque country has its own government. More than 2 million people live there, and the region is home to the world-famous Guggenheim Museum.

Spain is also home to many different regions that have their own language and culture. Many Spaniards choose to identify with the region they grew up in rather than the country of Spain itself. There are many regions such as Valencia, Catalonia, and the Basque country.

Pamplona is in the Basque country and the San Fermín festival is greatly influenced by the Basque people. Basque music is always played throughout the festival. There is *txistu* (a type of flute), *txalaparta* (an instrument similar to the xylophone), tambourines, and drums. There is also a Basque fair on July 6. There, people can watch Basque country sports, music, dances, and learn more about Basque culture.

A musician plays the Basque txistu.

Meaning

For some Spaniards, the San Fermín festival is about honoring the saint who gave his life to teach others about Christianity. When the runners line up at the starting line, they chant and pray to an image of San Fermín and ask him for his protection. It is one of the most emotional parts of the race because the runners know they are doing something dangerous and that one of them might not make it to the end of the race alive. After the songs and chants, the runners shout "Long live Saint Fermín!" first in Spanish and then in Basque.

Runners pray to Saint Fermín before running with the bulls.

The running of the bulls is about celebrating Spanish and Basque culture.

For most people, the festival is all about bringing people together, being proud of one's native country, showing bravery, and cherishing life. The festival has many fun things for people to do with their friends and family, like parades, fairs, and fireworks. Spaniards and Basques are very proud of their homeland, and there is folk music, dancing, and food during this time. The festival is also about realizing how important life is. As soon as the runners reach the finish line, some think about how close they were to death and are glad to glad to have reached safety.

DID YOU KNOW?

At the Plaza de los Fueros, there are traditional Basque sports such as stone lifting, haystack lifting, wood cutting, and Basque pelota. Basque pelota is a wall and ball game that is similar to racquetball.

Special Events

The race course starts on Santo Domingo street.

The running of the bulls takes place every morning of the San Fermín festival. It starts at 8 o'clock, at the **corral** in Calle Santo Domingo. There, the bulls wait at the gate to be released. The runners are at the starting line, chanting and singing. They wear traditional clothes: white shirts, red sashes, and red scarves. Soon, two shots are fired from a rocket gun. The bulls run out and the racers take off.

Runners run through a double fence made from thousands of wooden planks and posts, while cheering crowds watch from balconies above. The race is thrilling, but also very scary. Runners have to dodge charging bulls and sometimes get pushed and knocked down along the way. Many runners try to run faster than the bulls for the whole race, but sometimes the bulls are faster. When this happens, the runners in front are warned to move to the sidelines so the bulls can pass.

Thousands of people hold up their red scarves as rocket fire marks the start of the race.

Some runners are able to follow or run with the bulls all the way to the bullring. Once all the bulls are inside the ring, a third rocket is fired. The fourth rocket lets everyone know that the race is over. The runners celebrate and tell people about their adventure.

DID YOU KNOW?

Most runners carry a rolled up newspaper so that they can see how far they are from the bulls. The newspaper can also be used to drive the bulls away in case they get too close.

What Sets it Apart

The running of the bulls came from the bullfighting tradition. People needed to move the bulls from their corrals and into the ring for the fights with the matadors. Normally, drovers would drive the bulls from behind, but some people thought it was fun to run ahead of the bulls and try to beat them to the ring. Young men especially liked to prove how fast and brave they were. Over time, the running of the bulls became more popular, and now both men and women participate in the races.

Today, the running of the bulls is celebrated in Spain, Portugal, France, Colombia, Venezuela, Peru, Ecuador, Mexico, and the United States. There are also many other places around the world that have their own **version** of the bull run. Some people like the fun and excitement that comes from the bull runs, but they don't like the danger. There are runs where people use pigs, sheep, and bull costumes instead of real bulls.

Alaska has a reindeer run!

The running of the bulls is part of the bullfighting tradition.

DID YOU KNOW?

Running of the Red Bulls: In 2008, the energy drink company, Red Bull, had their own bull run at Pamplona. Instead of bulls, they used racing cars that chased runners through the streets.

Highlights

ROUTE LANDMARKS

Santo Domingo Street: The start of the bull run. There is a steep hill here and the bulls usually stay close together.

Plaza Consistorial-Mercaderes: A safe part of the race. It is wide and allows lots of room for people to run through. There are also many hiding places and safe spots from the bulls.

Bend of Estafeta: A dangerous corner where bulls sometimes slip and crash into the fence.

Bajada de Javier Street: A narrow path with few hiding places.

Stretch of Telefónica: A short running stretch. Runners and bulls become tired and begin to spread out.

Lane: A tunnel that leads into the bullring. It is dangerous because of the human pile-ups that can happen here.

Plaza de Toros: The bullring. Runners run to the sides of the circle while guides lead the bulls into pens. The race is over.

PASTORES AND DOBLADORES

Besides the runners, there are two groups of people that are important to the bull run. The first is the *pastores*, the bull herders. They run behind the bulls to make sure they keep moving in the right direction. Sometimes bulls get confused and move off course. This can be dangerous because they can crash into things and harm other people. The *pastores* have a long stick to move the bulls forward, and they also make sure that the other runners do not harm or upset the bulls.

The second group is the *dobladores*, the guides. They wear capes and wait for the runners and bulls to come to the bullring. Their job is to help the runners move to the sides of the ring and to get the bulls into the pens as quickly as possible. They use their capes to grab the bulls' attention and lead them away.

PARADE OF GIANTS

During the San Fermín festival, there is the *Comparsa de Gigantes,* or Parade of Giants. It is a parade with giant statues and bigheaded costumes. There are eight statues that are made from wood and dressed in fine clothing. They are statues of four kings and four queens, who each represent a different part of the world: Africa, America, Asia, and Europe. The statues are about 13 feet tall, and are carried on people's shoulders.

DID YOU KNOW?

The Comparsa de Gigantes statues were made by Pamplona artist Tadeo Amorena in 1860 and have been used ever since!

People in bigheaded costumes follow the kings and queens. They are the royal guards and servants. Their job is to protect the royal family. The *zaldikos* are also part of this group. They are people in half-men, half-horse costumes whose job is to scare and chase young children.

BULLFIGHTING

The morning bull runs lead to the evening bullfights. This is when the bulls from the run are released into the ring to fight a matador. Many people feel this is a cruel act, but for others it is an art like music or dancing.

The bullfight begins with a grand entrance. The matador is dressed up in 16th century Spanish fashion, with a gold-trim coat, **breeches**, and red stockings. After the matador come the other bullfighters and horsemen. Their job is to help the matador during the fight. The crowd claps and cheers and when a white handkerchief is thrown into the ring, the fight begins.

Around the World

Camargue, France
The small towns and villages of Camargue are dedicated to bulls. Bulls are part of life there and people have great respect for them. There is a summer bull festival each year with bull runs and other events in the streets.

Te Kuiti, New Zealand
In New Zealand, the town of Te Kuiti has a fake bull run with sheep instead of bulls. 2,000 sheep are released onto the main street with sheepdogs and people running alongside to make sure that the sheep move in the right direction.

New Orleans, Louisiana
New Orleans has a San Fermín festival with bull running, but instead of real bulls, the Big Easy Rollergirls wear bull costumes and chase runners with their roller skates. There are also other events such as music concerts, dance performances, and parties.

Ballyjamesduff, Ireland
Ballyjamesduff has a fake bull run with pigs instead of bulls. It is part of their yearly Pork Festival where people eat pork, have food contests, pig beauty contests, a sports competition called the Olympigs, and a Pig Latin competition.

The People

In Pamplona, 2,000 to 4,000 people run during each bull race. There are a total of eight morning bull runs throughout the whole San Fermín festival. Altogether, around 20,000 people take part in the Pamplona bull runs each year. Half of these runners are from Spain, while the rest are from different countries. About half of all runners are running with the bulls for the first time.

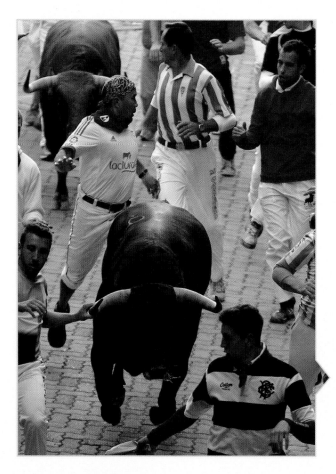

Throughout the years, some famous people have run with the bulls as well. Ernest Hemingway—an American author—visited the event many times, both as a watcher and as a runner. He is the one who made the running of the bulls world-famous by writing about the tradition in his book, *The Sun Also Rises* (called *Fiesta* in Spain). Recently, the New York Jets' coach, Rex Ryan, has also participated in the runs.

20,000 people run with the bulls each year.

The festival even has an Ernest Hemingway lookalike contest.

Impact

The running of the bulls makes Pamplona a very popular destination in Spain. In 2014, Spain had a record number of visitors. Over 8 million people came to visit and brought $35 million to Spanish restaurants, hotels, and stores. **Tourism** is very important to Spain because the country depends on tourist sales for jobs and financial support.

There are many things to see and do at the San Fermín festival. Every morning, people run with the bulls through the streets of Pamplona. You can watch from a balcony or behind the fence. After the run, you can listen to music or eat some local Spanish food. There are fun fairs with merry-go-rounds and carnival rides. Or you can head to the Plaza de los Fueros and watch the Basque country sports. The Parade of Giants also parades through the streets each day.

The last day of the festival is July 14. People gather at the City Hall Square with brightly lit candles. The mayor gives a speech and thanks everyone for coming to the party. Then fireworks light up the sky and people sing a goodbye song:

"Pobre de Mí, Pobre de Mí, que se han acabado las fiestas, de San Fermín."

Poor me, poor me, the San Fermín festival is over.

Celebrators say goodbye to the San Fermín festival.

Glossary

animal rights activist: someone who fights for the rights of animals

breeches: knee-length trousers that were commonly worn during the 16th to 19th centuries

bullfighting: a traditional Spanish sport where a bull is fought and killed by a matador

corral: a pen for cattle and horses

drovers: people who drive sheep or cattle from one location to another

fairs: events where farm products and food are sold; usually combined with entertainment and festivities

matadors: the main bullfighters in a bullfight

Middle Ages: the 6th to 16th centuries (500 to 1500 C.E.)

protest: to disagree with or fight against something you believe is wrong

Spaniards: people from Spain

tourism: the act of visiting or touring another location

tournaments: a test of skill in a game or competition; usually to win prizes

tradition: a set of beliefs and practices that are passed down from generation to generation

version: a different form or style; a different point of view

volunteers: people who help out the community without being paid